So What Do You Think?

A Guide to a Positive Mind

CLAIR SWINBURNE

iUniverse

So What Do You Think?
A Guide to a Positive Mind

iUniverse books may be ordered through booksellers or by contacting:

iUniverse
1663 Liberty Drive
Bloomington, IN 47403
www.iuniverse.com
1-800-Authors (1-800-288-4677)

ISBN: 978-1-4620-2935-8 (sc)
ISBN: 978-1-4620-2936-5 (hc)
ISBN: 978-1-4620-2937-2 (e)

Library of Congress Control Number: 2011909734

Print information available on the last page.

iUniverse rev. date: 05/29/2018

For my husband, my endless source of support & love

Contents

Part 1

Do You Know What You Want?	1
Who Do You Want To Be Like?	5
Who Is In Charge?	11
Anyone For An Attitude?	15
Are You Friends With You?	27
Do You Know What You're Doing When You're Doing It?	33
What Way Are You Seeing Things Today?	37
What Makes Up Your Reality?	41
What's Your Frequency, Kenneth?	49
In Your Mind, Are You Healthy?	57

Part 2

Awareness Is Key	71
Focus On What You Want	85

Part 1

Chapter 1

DO YOU KNOW WHAT YOU WANT?

"All of the animals except man, know that the principle business of life is to enjoy it"

Samuel Butler, poet

Let's start off by thinking about our ultimate aim here. Think about it for a second. What do we all ultimately want in life?

Many of you are probably thinking: Money!

Although that may be your first instinctive answer, it probably isn't ultimately what you want. Let's presume you are already rich. What would you then want in life?

Some of you are probably thinking: Success in your career!

Again, there's probably something else you're not thinking of. So let's assume you are rich and you have plenty of success in your career. Now, what do you think you want in life? Have we got there yet?

It's fair to say that everyone's ultimate aim in life is to be happy. We know that being rich doesn't make you happy. If it did, every wealthy person would be happy. But, of course, this is not the case. Also, it's not true that all people who are successful in their careers are happy.

Many of us get so distracted with the goals of money and work that sometimes we forget to give much attention or thought to how to achieve the most important thing in our lives, happiness.

Think about how much time you have ever devoted to your own happiness. Have you ever studied anything along those lines in school? Have you ever read any books that would enlighten you on the subject? Probably not.

In this book, we're going to analyse people who are happy and successful *in life*! This will give us an insight into what makes people happy and successful in everything they do. From this, we can learn new perspectives, strategies and attitudes which may improve our own wellbeing and produce more positive behaviour in us. We will also look at how our minds work to give us a clearer understanding of ourselves and our reality. This will give us a deeper knowledge about what works for us and what doesn't. Take on board the things that work for you.

I'll bet you've had this conversation with your mother when out shopping.

"I don't like that top."

"Try it on!"

"But I really don't like it!"

"Try it on!"

"But I'm not going to buy it since I don't like it, am I?"

"Try it on *for size*!"

I guess that's what I'm asking you to do. "Try things on for size!"

> *"If we all worked on the assumption that what is accepted as really true were really true, there would be little hope of advance"*
>
> *Orville Wright, inventor*

Chapter 2

WHO DO YOU WANT TO BE LIKE?

"If it's possible for anyone else to do, then it's possible to learn"

Anon

We often forget that this is true. If someone else can do something, then it *is* possible for us to learn how to do it too. Whatever you have admired in another person, did you realise that if they can do it, then you can learn it, too? You can learn anything, skills, attitudes, behaviours, perspectives ...

Think about someone who you think is truly happy. What characteristics and attitudes does that person have? Write them down. If a particular person doesn't spring to mind, think about what characteristics you would imagine a truly happy person to have?

Need a bit of help? In the 1970s, a group of psychologists asked themselves that same question. What characteristics do happy, successful people have? And what is it that works for them to produce excellent behaviour and a contentment that most people crave? This analysis became the foundation of what we now know as NLP.

NLP stands for **Neuro Linguistic Programming** and it is like an umbrella title for all things that work to produce successful and excellent behaviour. Most psychology studies look to analyse issues and focus on problem behaviours in order to understand how problems are developed. All the time and effort is focussed on the problem. NLP is refreshingly different in that it's not concerned with problem behaviours or analysing people's issues. NLP is all about focussing on *what works!*

As I mentioned earlier, it was developed by analysing successful and excellent behaviour in people who were experts in their field, were happy and successful in life, and who also brought about amazing positive change in others. They were analysed in terms of the thoughts and workings of their minds (neuro), the use of their language and their communication (linguistic), and the patterns of behaviour they consistently produced (programming).

We are all unique in so many different ways. This comes from what we learn from the world, from our experiences, from people in our lives, from our teachers, from our friends. But sometimes what we learn doesn't produce the best attitudes and strategies for happy successful lives and often we don't even realise it.

There is a great poem, 'Children Learn What They Live', by writer and family counsellor Dorothy Law Nolte (1924-2005) which really sums this up. Here's a snippet from it:

"If children live with criticism,
they learn to condemn.
...
If children live with fear,
they learn to be apprehensive"

We all learn different things and develop different ways of being. From our individual experiences, we develop strategies on how to live. We have developed strategies for everything: how to love, how to learn, how to cope, how to make a decision, how to *be*.

Some strategies work well for us and some don't work for us at all. Often, we don't even realise when something isn't working for us. We don't understand that some strategies we've picked up and learnt along the way may be completely ineffective and produce mediocre results. Life strategies or "techniques for becoming a happier person" aren't covered in school or in the majority of training courses. In many cases, we don't know about other strategies for life because we usually learn one way (from experience and people around us), and then we tend to stick with it, no longer "trying things on for size".

Think of the following example: You travel home from school or work a certain route every day. That works: You get to school or work every day. Then, one day, a friend tells you about the route she travels. Her way is quicker and there's less traffic on the roads! You had never even realised that there was a better road than the way you had been going for years. After all, you never had reason to question it; the route you took *did* get you to where you wanted to go. If you hadn't been talking to your friend about how you travel to work, you'd never have found out about the new quicker route. If she hadn't told you, then you'd never have known about it.

And that's true about life. We rarely chat and discuss life strategies with others. And we probably never think to question what the most effective ways of doing things are, to produce the best results for us? And if no one ever tells us, then how can we learn anything new?

We must be open to thinking about things in completely new ways. If we *start* thinking about these things, and looking at what other people do, and the strategies that clearly work for them, we can understand a little more about what might work better for us.

You may be very attached to some of your old ways of doing/thinking about things because you've been doing and thinking them for years, but that doesn't mean there aren't more effective ways out there. Often, when we see people doing something really well, we think, "Wow, that's great! But I could never do that; they can do it because it's who they are!"

Not true! Watch them, model them, do what they do. If it works for them, it may work for you too. After all, "If it's possible for anyone else to do, then it's possible to learn."

Chapter 3

WHO IS IN CHARGE?

"Everything that happens to us is the result of what we ourselves have thought, said, or done. We alone are responsible for our lives"

Buddha

One of the most important things to note about successful happy people is that they are on the 'Cause' side in life. What does this mean?

Psychologists say that we are either on the 'Cause' or the 'Effect' side in our approach to life. If you are on the 'Effect' side, you don't make positive changes in your life; only people on the 'Cause' side do. It is suggested that most people are on the 'Effect' side most of the time, but we can switch from one side to the other depending on different circumstances or times in our lives.

Examples:

Effect: "I didn't do well in my exams because my teachers were useless and my parents never pushed me to study!"

Cause: "I didn't do well in my exams because I didn't work as hard as I could have and I never studied."

Effect: "I didn't go for that job because Mary made me feel like I wouldn't be good enough."

Cause: "I didn't go for the job because I didn't take the opportunity."

Effect: "I can't pursue my dreams because my parents never taught me to put myself first."

Cause: "I am choosing not to pursue my dreams and in doing so I will teach my kids the same."

Figured out the difference? People on the 'Effect' side always blame other people, events and situations for why they did or did not do something. If it's always someone else's fault, then they never have to worry about taking charge or actually doing something about it themselves. However, they don't realise that by doing this, they give up control of their lives to other people, events and situations. Their doing something – anything - will depend on something someone *else* says or does.

If I asked you to give up the power to control your own life, would you agree? I didn't think so. But people forget that this is what they are effectively doing when they are on the 'Effect' side. People on the 'Cause' side accept responsibility for their actions. They understand that if they don't do something, the only people to blame are themselves.

Before you start thinking that being on the 'Cause' side means giving yourself a hard time about all the things you haven't done in your life, understand that it is also really empowering. Why? Because if you want to do anything in the future, you will also understand that it is you, and only you, who have the power to do it. You don't have to wait for other people or situations to align themselves before it can happen for you! People on the 'Effect' side see life as a game of chance. Certain things will happen and they can't do anything about it.

Successful happy people realise that we alone are responsible for our lives. There is so much in our lives that we *can* control. It is very comforting and empowering to know that *you* are in the driving seat of your own life. Thinking like this will automatically make you more likely to achieve goals you set in your future.

Think about it, if you ask most people how they ended up in their job, many of them will say that one thing led to another. They never thought that they would end up doing what they're doing. Many of us can be guilty of "reacting to situations". Being on the 'Effect' side of situations and people means we 'end up' in positions we'd never thought about or planned for. Sometimes, we "end up" in situations where we're very happy. However, you need to be aware of *when* you're letting people and situations direct your life and *when* you are taking responsibility and control of it yourself!

> **"You are in charge of your mind and therefore your results!"**
>
> **Anon**

It is also worth noting that the converse is true. When something goes well, we often tend to give the credit to other things or people. "I did really well in my exams because I had good teachers and my parents are the ones who pushed me to study." People can help us but it is ultimately *you* who does it. You should understand that when you do something good and positive in your life, it is *you* who should get the credit for it. We can often forget about that. Understanding that *you* are the cause of your achievements is a very important part of you learning to value and appreciate yourself.

And, of course, truly valuing and appreciating yourself makes you happy!

Chapter 4

ANYONE FOR AN ATTITUDE?

"Nothing can stop the man with the right mental attitude from achieving his goal; nothing on earth can help the man with the wrong mental attitude"

Thomas Jefferson, US President

In developing NLP, there were a number of common attitudes found amongst those people studied. Some of these attitudes were:

Respect for the other person's model of the world

We can't write people off because they don't match what we think they should be or do or think. We have all grown up in different situations and had different things to deal with throughout our lives. We've each had different experiences and influences. Naturally, this shapes the way we view the world. Even two brothers who are brought up by the same parents can still develop very different models and views of the world because no two people will ever have the same experiences or learning in their lives. Did you know that you are the only person who will ever *think* exactly as you do? It is important to remember this in order to help us better understand others and ourselves.

People are not their behaviours

People are so much more than their behaviours and it's very important to remember this when dealing with negative behaviours, especially our own. Everybody acts differently in different contexts and situations.

For example, when a person is really rude to you, your automatic reaction is to think that he is just a really rude person. However, their behaviour to you that day doesn't necessarily mean that is who they are. He could just be having a stressful day. His rude behaviour may have been completely out of character and just a by-product of a series of things that happened to him. Now, let's say he is regularly rude to people. It is important to understand (and respect his model of the world) that there could be many reasons why he has developed/ learned this behaviour. However, just because he was rude to you a number of times doesn't mean that he will *always* be rude, and it doesn't mean he will never be able to change that.

However, when people refuse to separate the person from the behaviour, they "label" the person. A label becomes an expectation (and hence a limitation) and, when we expect certain behaviours from people, we are rarely disappointed.

Labelling pupils regularly takes place in schools. Often, people don't even realise they are doing it; it's an unconscious reaction. When a pupil is acting out, being rude or aggressive, the pupil is often labelled by a teacher as a problem. It can often follow that the teacher will grow to expect that problem behaviour every time she is in the class. The pupil will often live up to these expectations. If the pupil wants to try and change their behaviour (but the teacher is expecting negative behaviour), they may not get the chance to change. And even if their behaviour does change, the teacher's perception might not.

There are numerous studies which support the fact that labels and expectations can be self-fulfilling prophecies. If you expect it, you get it! But there is a really interesting study by Carol S. Dweck, Ph.D. and Claudia M. Mueller, Ph.D.[1], which shows that even positive labels can have a negative effect. They found that even positively labelling a pupil's intelligence, for example using a label such as "gifted", can have a negative impact on a child's learning. How? It is found that pupils labelled "gifted" can often become reluctant to try new things for fear of making a mistake and doing something that might put that label into question. Not only do they demonstrate a reluctance

---

1   Mueller, Claudia M., Ph.D. & Dweck, Carol S., Ph.D (1998), "Praise for Intelligence Can Undermine Children's Motivation and Performance", Journal of Personality and Social Psychology, Vol. 75, No. 1

to try new things but also a real lack of coping skills if an attempt is then made but unsuccessful.

The psychologists found that commending pupils for their hard work and effort puts the focus on strategies for achievement rather than performance. If the pupil was unsuccessful, they blamed their own lack of effort or strategy rather than their intelligence. Dr. Dweck, Professor of Psychology at Stanford University and lead author of this study, says that the root of the problem lies not in the labels themselves but in the mind-sets they represent. Children who believe in permanent traits like fixed intelligence are actually vulnerable because, when something goes wrong, they think they don't deserve the label anymore, she says.

Alissa Quart, author of Hothouse Kids: The Dilemma of the Gifted Child[2], says the gifted label "fixes" children's identities into adulthood. While the label may be useful in education, it is not helpful as an internal self-image for the child.

In education, when there is a "learning disability", Dweck acknowledges that parents and children may be relieved to learn that there is a name for the problem and specific remedies. However, a learning disability, she said, does not mean that a child can't learn. However, parents need to explain to their children that different strategies and harder work may be required for the child to get by in school. Regardless of the intelligence or the issue,

---

2   Quart, Alissa (2007), <u>Hothouse Kids: The Dilemma of the Gifted Child</u>, Penguin (London)

Dweck insists that when children are taught the value of "concentrating, strategising, and working hard" when dealing with academic challenges, this encourages them to sustain their motivation, performance, and self-esteem.

This further confirms that, when we use labels, we create limitations. It is the mindset that is connected to the label that is always the issue.

There is no such thing as failure, only feedback

What do you think of when you hear the word "failure"? Successful happy people don't think about failure in the same way as most. They view disappointments or setbacks as learning opportunities.

Let's view this in terms of tests in school. Often, when a pupils "fails" a test, they tend to take this on board at an identity level. They see the score and directly translate it into, "I am a failure". Happy, successful people see test scores/criticism/rejection as *feedback* and *learning* instead of confirmation of things they cannot do or achieve. Did you know Lord Alan Sugar from the UK TV show, 'The Apprentice', was bankrupt *twice*? Even when he went bankrupt the second time, he didn't let that change who he knew he could be. It only made him more determined. Now, he's worth an estimated £800 million.

"Success seems to be connected with action. Successful people keep moving. They make mistakes but don't quit"

Conrad Hilton, businessman

When you were first learning to walk and you fell down a few times, your parents didn't go, "Aw that's it, he tried it but it's obvious this one just ain't gonna be a walker, we may as well forget about it!"

> **"Anyone who has never made a mistake has never tried anything new"**
>
> **Albert Einstein, physicist and mathematician**

Everything in your life is feedback! When something doesn't work out, learn what *not* to do next time. When viewing things in this way, wonderful things can happen. So many of people's success stories have similar threads to Lord Alan Sugar's. In fact, almost all of them do!

So, do you see setbacks, failures or criticisms as confirmations of who you are? Or, do you decide to learn from those mistakes and use the feedback as an opportunity to grow and improve.

The map is not the territory

The words we use aren't always the item or event they represent.

Let me explain. I usually split a class up into groups of about four. I ask them to each write down the first three things that come into their head when I say a certain word. Then I ask them if there's a match in the group.

For it to be a match, every other person at the table must have written down the same word.

The interesting thing is that we rarely get a match in the group. This shows that our minds all work in very different ways. Words conjure up different memories and associations in people. Language is just a way of communicating what's going on inside our heads. It's a structure we use to try and verbalise our thoughts and, like any structure, it has its limitations. Have you ever been in a situation where you just couldn't find the right words to explain what it was that was going on inside your head? Or there were no words to describe exactly what it was you were feeling? The words we use don't give the full story sometimes. So, it's important to remember that, often, what you *actually* say mightn't be exactly what you *mean* and, also, what you say mightn't be what others *hear.* Think of it like this. You could represent London using a Tube map. Or an A-Z road map. They are both maps, both representations of London, both correct. But they are both different and both are not quite complete representations of the whole city.

So why is this important to remember in terms of our attitudes and beliefs? It's important to always delve a little deeper when thinking about situations or, especially, misunderstandings. Never react solely on what someone has said because, more than likely, what they've *said* isn't what they've *meant*. Especially, don't get caught up with what someone has told you someone has said, because that will definitely be a distorted message. So many arguments arise out of miscommunication and somebody doing or saying something with both parties taking things up the wrong way. Always be prepared to get to the bottom of what really happened before flying off the handle or reacting straight away to a situation. What we say isn't always what we really mean to say or, perhaps, what others actually hear!

Everyone is doing the best they can with the resources they have available

Sometimes, we need to just give ourselves a break. We often cling onto "shoulda, woulda, coulda". "I should have done this, I could have said that." We all do the best we can at any one time. With hindsight, it's a lot easier to think about how to handle a situation. You have to remember that you did the best you could at that time with the skills and resources you had at that time.

Everybody else does the same, so be wary of judging other people on what they do or how they cope. Everyone has different backgrounds, memories, associations and learning. Other people may not have the same skills or resources as you for dealing with or handling certain things. So, if you want to help others, don't judge. Respect their model of the world and help them improve their skills and increase their resources or their 'life tool box'. View everything as feedback, don't dwell on it - learn from it. Increase your resources and improve your skills for the next time something comes your way.

The more flexible the behaviour, the more likely the positive outcome

Here are a set of images that demonstrates this point really well.

"If you always do what you've always done, then you'll always get what you always got!"

Anon

If you're not prepared to be flexible with your behaviour, how can you expect a different outcome? If something doesn't work for you, stop doing it. Change it! The problem is, we can be stubborn and continue to do the same things even though they don't work for us. We become set in our ways and habits and are unwilling to try something new or even attempt a different approach. However, if we have an attitude of seeing everything as feedback rather than failure, and are willing to be flexible in our approach to things, then we are far more likely to get the results we want. Some of you mightn't be familiar with this but a great example of flexible behaviour is one that appeared in a TV advert for Vicks. (Try finding it on www.youtube.com and type in "Vick's first defence tantrum"). The mother is in the shop with her little boy and the scenario unfolds where the little boy goes straight for the treats to put them in the trolley. When she says no, he starts having a tantrum. What's the usual response to this behaviour? Probably a whole argument and a sulking child! However, instead of reacting how mothers usually react, she gets down on the floor and has a tantrum herself. The child is so surprised with his mother's behaviour he just drops the treats and carries on shopping. Her flexible behaviour brought about the quickest, most effective positive response. The child, completely stunned out of his normal pattern of behaviour, just drops the treats and carries on. No arguments, no fighting, no sulking!

> *"I can't change the direction of the wind, but I can adjust my sails to always reach my destination"*
>
> *James Dean, actor*

Chapter 5

ARE YOU FRIENDS WITH YOU?

"We have to learn to be our own best friends because we fall too easily into the trap of being our own worst enemies"

Roderick Thorp, writer

A teacher says to a young student,

"You are wonderful, you are doing great! You are really really intelligent! You are beautiful today; now off you go and have a good day!"

What effect would this have, do you think, on that student if they heard this *every* morning for a number of weeks?

Now, imagine if the first thing a teacher said to that student each morning was,

"You are useless! You look a disgrace! You are so stupid and pathetic! You're just ridiculous! Now off you go about your day."

Ok, I'm being dramatic with the sentences here, for effect, but you get the idea of the scenarios. I think we'd all agree that the negative impact would be very apparent in the student's attitude and behaviour, if a person of authority and influence, spoke in that way, on a regular basis, to a student. In this example, it's clear to understand the effect of the negative comments.

Now, let's personalise it. How do *you* chat to *yourself?* We all have a voice chatting to us inside our heads, commenting, criticising, cajoling. Can your mental chatter sound like that second teacher sometimes? Have you said a number of negative things to yourself already today? You're probably thinking, "OK, I do sometimes have a go at myself, but I don't do it all the time". Sometimes, my mental chatter is like the first teacher and, sometimes, it's more like the second.

Now, imagine if your teacher said you were wonderful and intelligent and beautiful one day. The next, she says you're useless, a disgrace, pathetic. One day, she builds you up; the next day, she slates you. What's the impact now? Is it positive or negative? Which will you remember – the compliment or the criticism?

We often don't realise that mixed messages are just as damaging as continuous negative ones. We give ourselves mixed messages all the time without realising the damage that *we* are doing to *ourselves*. How can you expect to become the best possible version of you if you talk to yourself in a way that you know can only have a negative impact on your attitude and behaviour?

> *"The way you treat yourself sets the standard for others"*
>
> **Dr Sonya Friedman, psychologist**

There is some fascinating work by Masaru Emoto, an internationally renowned Japanese author and researcher, which poses some really interesting questions. His vast research visually captures the structure of water at the moment of freezing using high-speed photography. Water, at the moment of freezing, creates a crystalline structure. Masaru Emoto found that he could never find two photos where the crystalline structures looked the same, even though the water used and the procedures followed were identical.

He found this really interesting and wanted to investigate what things affected the crystalline structures. He found many fascinating differences when he subjected the water to different environments or conditions. Water is a very malleable substance. Its physical shape easily adapts to the surrounding environment. The molecular shape also changes. Clean, unpolluted water showed beautiful geometric designs when photographed at the moment of freezing. Polluted water produced distorted and randomly formed crystalline structures.

Masaru Emoto decided to see how thoughts and words affected the formation of untreated, distilled water using words typed onto paper by a word processor. The labels were left on the samples overnight. The effect was truly astounding.

Words like Love, Peace, and Thank You created beautiful, crystalline structures whereas phrases such as, "You make me sick, I will kill you", and "You fool" created deformed and yellow effects on the crystals.

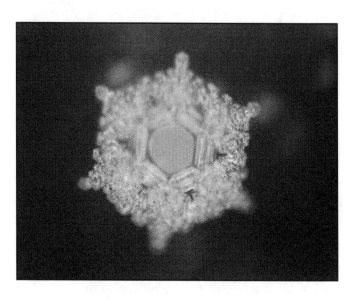

Love and Gratitude
credit © Office Masaru Emoto, LLC

Thank You
credit © Office Masaru Emoto, LLC

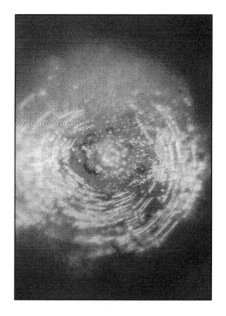

You Fool
credit © Office Masaru Emoto, LLC

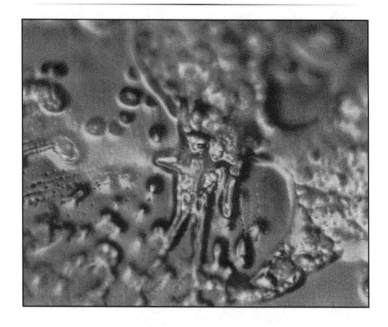

You Make Me Sick I Will Kill You
credit © Office Masaru Emoto, LLC

The results are amazing. But the most significant thing about all his research is that if thoughts and words have such a profound effect on water, what impact can thoughts and words have on us? After all, our bodies are over 70 per cent water.

So, if you ever thought that the mental chatter inside your head is unimportant, think again. It affects you hugely. In fact, it is THE most important thing and it affects everything in your life.

> **"You are what you think about all day long"**
>
> **Dr. Robert Schuller, pastor and author**

Chapter 6

DO YOU KNOW WHAT YOU'RE DOING WHEN YOU'RE DOING IT?

"What you are aware of, you are in control of. What you are unaware of, is in control of you"

Anthony de Mello, Jesuit priest and psychotherapist

Have you ever woken up in a good mood? You feel good, refreshed, and happy. Your day proceeds nicely until you sit down to chat with a friend. He's not having a good day and tells you all about it. On and on, you listen to how he's had an argument with his brother, how everyone is against him lately, how unfair life is for him right now. You part company and you find yourself scolding/criticising the next person you meet. And the next. Where has your good mood gone?

It is very easy to take on board someone else's mood without even realising it. We often don't understand how easy it is to lose control of our own emotional state by being so easily influenced by somebody else.

If you tune into your moods, you will be able to see whether you allow certain things and people to influence them. When a shift in your mood occurs, retrace your thoughts to the thought or incident that brought about a change in your feelings. This can often reveal that the intensity of the feeling is now no longer there. Although the feeling is correctly associated with that particular thought, the intensity is no longer the same. Your brain has rationalised the feeling, even though the original feeling and shift in mood happened just moments earlier. When unaware of the actual thought or incident that shifted your mood, you continue with the new mood with no understanding of where it came from or the necessity for it.

Becoming more aware will show you how influenced we can be by other people's energies and states. This awareness will enable you to stay in control of your state, regardless of whom you are with. Ask yourself, is the mood your own and is it necessary? Remember, you are in charge of your moods and you have the power to redirect your thoughts to keep yourself in a positive state, if you so wish. Contrary to what you probably think, *you* have the power to choose your thoughts. Although you might feel at times that this is not the case, know that if a thought jumps into your head, *you choose* whether to keep thinking that thought or to change the thought to something else. When you are in control of your mind, you are in control of your state.

"You are in charge of your mind and therefore your results"

Anon

Chapter 7

WHAT WAY ARE YOU SEEING THINGS TODAY?

"We don't see things as they are; we see things as we are"

Anais Nin, author

If there was a mugging on the street and a witness saw the whole event, would the police have ample evidence to prosecute the mugger when caught?

Years ago, it was generally assumed that an eyewitness' testimony would be sufficiently accurate to be used as sole evidence for prosecution in a case. However, after a number of cases where identity parades led to the mis-identification of a suspect, the publication of the Devlin Report[3] in 1976 in the UK led to changes in the way eyewitness testimonies were viewed. The Devlin Report and further studies by psychologists have shown

---

3   Devlin Committee Report: Report of the Committee on Evidence of Identification in Criminal Cases, (1976) Cmnd 338 134/135, 42

that not only are witnesses often inaccurate in their memory of people and events, but there is also often little relationship between the accuracy of their recall and their level of confidence about what they saw. Leading questions by an interviewer can play a part in the distortion of a person's recall, however; there is no denying that when different people observe an event, they see different things. Buckhout (1980) conducted a study[4] with 2000 participants. A 13-second film was shown on prime-time TV. Later, an identity parade was shown on TV and viewers were invited to phone in their choice of suspect based on the film. Only 14 per cent got it right.

Why is it that two people can observe the exact same scenario but yet describe the event in very different ways?

It is reported that there are 400 billion bits of information coming at you every second. That's way too much information for your brain to be able to digest. So your brain is forced to delete, distort and generalise the information, so that you can perceive it. First, your brain will delete a whole chunk of the information based on what is not relevant to you. It's said that we only absorb 2,000 bits of information every second. So, there are lots of bits of information that you are not even processing.

Based on your own beliefs, experiences and attitudes, you generalise the rest of the information. Just like the

4   Buckhout, R. (1980), 'Nearly 2000 witnesses can be wrong'. Bul-letin of Psychonomic Science, Vol 16, p307–10

pessimist sees the glass as half-empty and the optimist sees it as half-full, your own way of thinking will distort the bits of information that you actually do process. You cannot perceive anything that is outside of yourself. So, how we see things reflects who we are and how we think.

> **"People seem not to see that their opinion of the world is also a confession of character"**
>
> **Ralph Waldo Emerson, poet**

This old story is a great example of how, regardless of a change in circumstances, a perception will remain the same if the attitude remains the same.

A man was travelling from one town to another when he met an old man sitting on a rock at the side of the road. Wanting to know about the people in the town he was travelling to, he stopped and asked the old man, "What are the people like in the next town?"

The old man looked up and asked, "How did you find the people in the town from which you came?"

The traveller answered, "Oh, they were wonderful, kind, courteous and friendly!" The old man said, "Well, you'll find the people the very same in the next town."

The next day, another man was travelling to the town when he met the same old man at the side of the road.

Also, wanting to know about the people in the town he was travelling to, he stopped and asked the old man, "What are the people like in the next town?"

The old man looked up and asked, "How did you find the people in the town from which you came?" "Oh, they were terrible, the meanest, most unfriendly people that you could meet"

The old man looked at him and said, "I'm afraid you will find the people in this town the same."

> **"If you do not see God in the next person you need, you need look no further"**
>
> **Gandhi**

When we point a finger at someone else, we always have three fingers pointing back at ourselves. This is to remind us that if we see something in someone else, it says more about us than it does about the other person.

If each of us perceives things differently, that begs the question, how do we know what is *actually* happening? We are always just getting people's versions of *their* reality, and each version will always be distorted by *their* own experiences and attitudes.

> **"We don't live in a world of reality; we live in a world of perceptions"**
>
> **Gerald J. Simmons**

Chapter 8

WHAT MAKES UP YOUR REALITY?

"The difference between fiction and reality? Fiction has to make sense"

Tom Clancy, novelist

We've looked at how our mental chatter and thoughts affect our own behaviour and how being in control of it will affect not only *our behaviour* but *our state*. And, we also looked at how our attitudes and beliefs affect how we actually *perceive the world*. But can our thoughts and beliefs actually affect what circumstances we see?

Here's the science bit!

In the 2004 film, 'What the Bleep Do We Know?', Dean Radin, senior scientist at the Institute of Noetic Sciences, California, discusses a very important but simple study. It's a study that has been conducted hundreds of times over the past four decades and involves random number generators. A random number generator is a device that will produce a sequence of numbers and the numbers that show up are completely... you guessed it ... random. The particular random number generator used in all of these experiments just produced zeros or ones. A person was asked to press a button on the random number generator to get the device to produce 200 numbers randomly. Then, the person was asked to try and get the device to produce more one numbers than zero numbers. The purpose was that the person would try to *intend* or *will* the device to produce more one numbers.

Amazingly, the intention of the person pressing the button has an effect on the results that appear. If the person thinks and wishes for more ones, the generators produce more ones. Crazy, right? So, why is this study so significant?

If this is true, it has a profound impact on the way we should think about things. *How* can your thoughts or intentions *actually* have an impact on what happens? Mysterious, invisible connections don't work like that in the world of science! Do they?

Let's look into it a bit more.

The study of reality and what affects it has kept scientists busy since the beginning of time. It's the age-old question, what is reality? What affects it? It has baffled the likes of Galileo, Newton, Descartes and Einstein! Scientists have made amazing discoveries when trying to get to the bottom of this particular question. So, like any complex problem, the best way to understand it is to break it down.

This is exactly what the scientists did. In order to try and understand how reality really worked, they began to break it down to see what happened on a much smaller scale.

Take matter, it's real and it's solid and it's what makes up our world. The key question for years has been, 'What makes up our matter?' When you break it down, you find that matter is made up of atoms. So we're talking about things that are very small here. There are metres, then smaller again are centimetres (cm), then millimetres (mm). Atoms are almost the equivalent of 0.0000001cm,[5] if you can even imagine something that small! Scientists thought that once they could understand what goes on at this level, the same laws would apply to (our normal) larger level. Makes sense, right?

Wrong!

According to Stuart Hameroff M.D. (Professor of Anaesthesiology and Psychology at the University of Arizona), "the universe is very strange". He says that, when you get down to the level of atoms (in other words, really small!), a whole different set of laws govern our world. In other words, things do not behave in the way scientists thought they would. When things are roughly in our normal size and time scale, we have

---

5 Holtzclaw, Henry F. & Robinson, William R. (1988). General Chemistry. Heath. (Lexington, MA)

laws of motion and gravity, and so on. However, when we get down to the level of atoms, in other words the Planck scale (the smallest level of reality), the laws of motion and gravity do not work the same. In fact, a whole different set of laws take over. Scientists call these the quantum laws (quantum mechanics and quantum physics). At this really small level, atoms and particles can be in multiple places at once (Superposition). And, at this level, particles can be interconnected over great distances (Entanglement).

Here's a great experiment about Entanglement at work. I discovered it through reading about multi-millionaire John Assaraf. Like a lot of really successful people, he uses the attitudes and techniques discussed in this book but never really understood *why* they worked. When he was younger, he just didn't really care. He quickly learned from observing happy successful people what seemed to work to produce these great results. He always just copied what they did, practised the techniques and reaped the rewards without thinking too much more about it. However, later on in life, after he gained financial freedom and had achieved great successes in business, he found himself wanting to pursue the 'science' behind it all. He became really intrigued about *why* the techniques and attitudes he had learnt worked. When doing his research on how our reality works, he came across a very interesting study describing the law of Entanglement in quantum physics.

Physicist Irwin Laslow in his book, Science and the Akashic Field[6], describes an experiment conducted by polygraph expert Cleev Baxter. Baxter took some white blood cells from the mouths of his participants and cultured them in a test tube. He then moved these test tubes over seven miles away from his laboratory and attached polygraphs to them. A polygraph, more familiarly known as a lie detector, is an instrument that monitors a person's physiological reactions. He then returned to his lab to conduct a series of tests on the participants. In one of his tests, he showed one of his participants, a former navy man, a television programme. The programme was on the Japanese attack on Pearl Harbour and the navy man had actually been present during this attack. During the programme, the navy man's face appeared on the screen and the man obviously had an emotional reaction to seeing himself. At the precise moment that he reacted to seeing his own face appear before him, the polygraph's needle over seven miles away jumped. It was as if the polygraph was attached to the man himself and not just to a test tube of his cultured white blood cells miles away.

Einstein called this, "Spooky action at a distance"! In the world of quantum physics, the particles of the navy man's body are still connected or entangled with one another; no matter how far apart they are separated by space, they will always continue to influence one another.

6   Laszlo, Ervin (2004), <u>Inner Traditions, Science and the Akashic Field</u>, Rochester (Vermont)

"As far as the laws of mathematics refer to reality, they are not certain; and as far as they are certain, they are not reality"

Albert Einstein, physicist and mathematician

So, why all this talk about quantum laws?

It's important to realise that the things you probably took for granted, that you probably thought were certain and fact in this world, actually stem from scientific quantum principles that are truly extraordinary. Science actually supports the fact that the world is wonderful and weird. An open mind is the only way to understand the amazing scientific process that describes what affects our reality. And so, to truly understand this, let's go a little deeper into understanding of what our reality is made up!

Phoebe, from one of the most popular sitcoms ever made, 'Friends'[7], brings up the next important fact I want to share with you about atoms.

> Phoebe and Ross are fighting because she doesn't 'buy into' the theory of evolution!
>
> Phoebe: Uh-oh, it's scary, scientist man.
>
> Ross: OK, Phoebe, this is it! In this briefcase, I carry actual scientific facts. A briefcase of facts, if you will. Some of these fossils are over two hundred million years old.

7　US TV sitcom aired on NBC from 1994 to 2004

Phoebe: OK, look, before you even start, I'm not denying evolution; I'm just saying that it's one of the possibilities.

Ross: It's the *only* possibility, Phoebe.

Phoebe: OK, Ross, can you just open your mind, like, this much? Wasn't there a time when the brightest minds in the world believed that the earth was flat? And up until, like, 50 years ago, you all thought the atom was the smallest thing until you split it open and this whole mess of crap came out! Now, are you telling me that you are so unbelievably arrogant that you can't admit that there's a teeny tiny possibility that you could be wrong about this?

Ross (after a considerable pause): There might be … a teeny…tiny…possibility.

Phoebe: I can't believe you caved!

Ross: What??!?

Phoebe: You just abandoned your whole belief system! Before, I didn't agree with you but at least I respected you. Now, how are you going to go into work tomorrow? How are you going to face the other science guys? How are you going to face yourself?

Ross leaves.

Phoebe was right! Up until about 50 years ago or, more accurately, the turn of the Twentieth Century, scientists thought atoms were the smallest articles that made up our reality until they split one open and "a whole mess of crap came out"! Walton, Cockroft and Rutherford were reported to be the first scientists to split the atom and verify Einstein's famous formula: $e=mc^2$ (energy equals mass times the speed of light squared). This describes to us how energy and matter are not only related but how they can be transformed back and forth into each other. This basically means that atoms can be broken down and inside atoms they found- Energy. The further we break down our reality, the more we realise that *everything* is made up of illusive little packets of *energy*. With his famous formula, Einstein was the first to realise this. Everything is made up of energy!

As John Assaraf explains, "A rock, a planet, a glass of water, your hand, everything you can touch, taste or smell, it's all made up of molecules"[8]. Molecules are made up of atoms. Atoms are made up of protons, electrons and neutrons. And they are made up of nothing but vibrating vortices of energy. So, there is no absolute distinction between matter and energy.

Everything is energy.

---

8   Assaraf, John [and Murray Smith] (2008), <u>The Answer</u>, Simon & Schuster Ltd (New York)

Chapter 9

WHAT'S YOUR FREQUENCY, KENNETH?

"You are like a human transmission tower, transmitting a frequency with your thoughts. If you want to change anything in your life, change the frequency by changing your thoughts"

Rhonda Byrne, author of The Secret

Since everything in our reality is made up of energy, it's important to understand how energy works and what affects it, right?

Bruce H. Lipton Ph.D., in his book, The Biology of Belief[9], says, "Physical atoms are made up of vortices of energy. Because each atom has its own specific energy signature, assemblies of atoms (molecules) collectively radiate their own identifying energy patterns. So, every

---

9 Lipton, Bruce, <u>The Biology of Belief</u>, (2008) Hay House Inc. (Carlsbad)

material structure in the universe, including you and me, radiates a unique energy signature."

Everything is energy and energy emits a certain signature or frequency.

We are energy and, hence, *we* emit a certain frequency!

You don't have to be a psychic to feel these different energy frequencies; we all feel it! Have you ever walked into a room and "felt" the tension? That's the energy in the room you're feeling. Have you ever sat down beside someone and just known they were in a horrible mood without him or her saying a single word to you? That's their energy you're feeling. People emit different energies/frequencies all the time and we *all* can feel and sense it.

How come bullies in school never go near the girls (or boys) who will fight back? Because, even if it's their first time meeting you, they'll know from your energy/ frequency whether they'd get away with bullying you or not! Every thought you think broadcasts a frequency. And people respond to your frequency without them or you even realising it. Did you know that when you communicate with someone, the words you use only account for about 30 per cent of the communication? Your "frequency" and the "vibes" you give off through your body language and voice tone account for the vast majority of the communication.

"99% of who you are is invisible and untouchable"

R. Buchminster Fuller, inventor

Now, here's a very important point you need to know: frequencies vibrate on certain wavelengths and, because of that, we are attracted to people and events on similar wavelengths to us. This is where the Law of Attraction comes from. If you have read the book or watched the film, 'The Secret', you will be familiar with this concept.

Let's recap. Rhonda Byrne's book, The Secret[10], explains to us that we get in life what we focus on. We *attract* everything into our lives. Our thoughts emit a certain frequency and because of that, certain people or situations are attracted to us. It works on the principle that like attracts like, but on the level of energies and thoughts. Our thoughts have energy. Every thought emits a certain frequency and can be measured. It has now been scientifically proven and measured that an affirmative and positive thought is hundreds of times more powerful than a negative thought. According to The Secret, the law of attraction says that if you're thinking about a certain thought over and over again, then you're sending out a magnetic signal that is drawing the parallel back to you. Summed up, it basically says, "Thoughts Create Things!"

---

10   Byrne, Rhonda (2006), <u>The Secret,</u> Simon & Schuster Ltd (New York)

Here's the problem. Most people think about and concentrate on what they *don't* want. And then they wonder why it shows up over and over again. The film, 'The Secret', teaches us that the law of attraction doesn't care whether you perceive something to be good or bad or whether you don't want it or whether you do want it. It's responding to your thoughts. Whatever it is you're focussing on, you will get more of! So if you're thinking things like, "I have no money, I can't afford that", "I can't study" or "People always pick on me", and you're feeling really bad about it, that's the signal you are putting out to the universe. If you're thinking those thoughts regularly, you are just affirming to yourself what you don't want or don't have. You feel it on every level of your being and, by emitting that frequency, that's what you get more of.

> *"You attract to you the predominant thoughts that you're holding in your awareness whether those thoughts are conscious or unconscious"*
>
> *Rev. Dr. Michael Beckwith, visionary*

Sound a bit hard to digest?

John Assaraf, in his book, The Answer,[11] says that one of the main things at work in the law of attraction is the scientific law, the Law of Resonance. He explains that resonance, from the Latin meaning "to sound again", is simply the transfer of vibration from one medium to

11   Assaraf, John [and Murray Smith] (2008), The Answer, Simon & Schuster Ltd (New York)

another. Have you ever wondered why a singer hitting a certain note can shatter glass? According to John, if you were to lightly strike that specific piece of glass with a tiny hammer, it would ring out a tone with the same pitch as the singer's high note. That's because the singer's high note and the glass share the same waveform, which is why they resonate. The same applies to thoughts. If the right thought is held clearly and strongly enough, it can influence physical events. "The principle of resonance says that energy, in a specific pattern or frequency, will resonate with every other form of energy in a similar pattern," says John.

This basically means that your energy will resonate with people and situations on the same wavelength as your frequency. Your thoughts are what makes you, you. How you think makes up your personality, attitude and character. Your "energy" comes from your thoughts and, so, how you think determines what kind of people and situations will resonate with you or be attracted to you.

Think about some situations you may have already come across in your life which help you to understand this law at work. Consider the bullying example from before. It is so true that bullies often just know who they can bully. They pick up straight away on a person's frequency or wavelength, if you like.

Here's an example of the Law of Resonance at work from my own life.

When I worked in a school in London, a few weeks into one school year, a new boy arrived. He was young and in the first year of secondary school, but had already been expelled from a previous secondary school in a different area, in a very short space of time. My colleagues on the pastoral team and I were, of course, very concerned about the boy. He was so young to be getting into such trouble.

The morning he arrived, we had him in classes with some really great teachers and had some of our best boys showing him around, being his "buddy" for the day. At break, a number of the teachers and I were in the staff room discussing the new boy. The staff room overlooked the playground, which meant we could keep an eye on the kids during break and lunch. This particular morning, as you can imagine, we were keeping a very close eye on the new boy.

Here's the really interesting thing. Within seven minutes in the playground, all the "boldies" from the older year groups had starting chatting to him. We couldn't believe it! All our planning to keep him with good influences but we hadn't accounted for the law of resonance at work. In a matter of minutes, the "boldies" in the school were drawn to the boy. Unconsciously, they were attracted to his frequency and recognised that he was on the same wavelength as them. This all happened without their conscious awareness and at a speed that would astonish you.

Have you ever been thinking about someone you haven't seen in a while and then, a couple of days later, you hear some information about that person or you end up getting a call from them? No? Then try it. Start thinking about someone and focus your energy and thoughts on him or her and see what happens.

As John Assaraf suggests, a thought (or energy wave form) held clearly and strongly enough will cause things in the physical world to be drawn/attracted to us, since things in the physical world are made up of energy and this is how energy works. Think of another simple energy form, a ray of light. If a ray of light is strong enough, and correctly focussed and concentrated, it can cause a piece of paper to catch fire. That just shows how much power an energy form has. Our thoughts are made up of that very same energy form! And, they too, have amazing strength and power.

Have you ever wondered why there are certain things that *never* come into your experiences but, for others, they happen all the time? Why do certain people always seem to have dramas after dramas? How come everything is a struggle for some people but it all falls into place for others? If their thoughts are emitting a frequency, wavelength, belief or expectation over and over, then that is what will resonate with them and be drawn into their world.

Now that you are aware of this, you will start to see it more and more in your life. It truly is remarkable how certain situations, people or opportunities come into our lives. Some people call it luck (good/bad) or coincidences.

When you understand how this works, you can really, truly gain control of your life and your future.

> **"You create your own universe as you go along"**
>
> *Winston Churchill (1874-1965), UK statesman*

So, here's the all-important question: Do you even *know* what type of frequency you emit on a regular basis? Do you truly know what your unconscious and automatic thought responses are to things? Are they negative and always expecting the worst or is there a "knowingness" that everything will be fine?

It's hard to monitor your thoughts all the time, you have so many. The easiest thing to do is to be aware of your feelings. Your feelings will reflect to you what kind of thoughts you have been thinking.

> *"Your feelings tell you very quickly what you are thinking. Think about when your feelings suddenly took a dive - maybe when you heard some bad news. Your feelings are an immediate signal for you to know what you are thinking. You want to become aware of how you are feeling and get in tune with how you're feeling, because it is the fastest way for you to know what you're thinking"*
>
> *Rhonda Byrne, author of The Secret*

Chapter 10

IN YOUR MIND, ARE YOU HEALTHY?

"Every human being is the author of his own health or disease"

Buddha

Any doctor or nurse will tell you that, when dealing with patients in recovery, they can never say with any certainty how long recovery may take after an operation. They will also tell you that one of the most important factors in a patient's recovery will be the patient's *attitude* to their recovery. It is seen time and time again in hospitals. Different patients, although perhaps very similar in age and health, can differ dramatically in how they recover after the same procedure. It is also seen time and time again in hospitals, amazing unexplainable recoveries. Recoveries never conceived possible. What is the explanation behind these? God? Fate? Miracles?

Psychologists have carried out many studies into how our beliefs and attitudes affect our healing. There have been so many studies, in fact, that there's now an "effect" to describe how *belief* is a powerful medicine. It is of course the "Placebo Effect." Take two groups of people suffering from a similar ailment, Group A and Group B. Both groups are told that they will be given medication to cure the ailment. However, in actual fact, only Group A will receive the medication. Group B receives a pill that is a vitamin or something that will have no physical effect on them. However, Group B *believes* it to be the medication. Now, here's the really interesting part. Over and over, given the many times this study has been replicated, the findings are extraordinary. In Group B, many patients show the same if not better recoveries than those in Group A. How is this possible?

"The Placebo Effect" shows us that our minds are very much connected with our bodies. This is a concept that people in western society don't fully accept yet. However, what is very strange is that, it *is* accepted on certain levels but just not all.

For example, everyone agrees that stress has an effect on our immune system, leading to ulcers, heart attacks, heart disease and so on. Well, what is stress? It's hard to say because there is no particular definition that describes what stress is. Different **things** stress out different people. So, we can't describe stress as a **thing**. How can we best describe it? I guess, stress is something we **feel**. How do you feel when you're stressed? Overwhelmed, under pressure, panicky? Are we saying that the decrease in immune functioning and all these known stress-related illnesses are caused by *feelings*? Most people in western society dismiss this connection completely, but why? How else can you explain what stress is?

Let's think about another aspect for a second. *Why* do we feel pain? Why do we live in a world where we must feel pain? Wouldn't it be great if you didn't ever have to feel sore or have an ache or be sick? But what would happen if you fell and broke your leg but you didn't feel it? Yes, the dangling wonky leg might give it away! But, say you injured yourself internally and had no idea because you felt no pain. We feel pain for a very important reason. It is the body's way of telling you that something needs attention. Your body is a feedback mechanism; it tells you when something is not quite right.

Your body is amazing! Think about what it does. Think of your unconscious mind, for example. Your unconscious mind is a term to describe all that goes on in your mind without your conscious awareness. It is your unconscious mind that helps run your body. Think about all the things your body does without you even knowing it. You breathe unconsciously, your heart beats, your body takes your nutrients from your food and delivers it to wherever it needs to go, and it gets rid of toxins in your body. All of this goes on without you even knowing it. Your body is a healing machine! When you cut yourself, what does it do? It heals itself. Your body was designed to work that way. However, if your body is under any "stress", it cannot do what it was designed to do. But, if your body is under "stress", we are talking about your body experiencing negative feelings, aren't we?

Are there really physical responses to how we *feel*? Well, of course, there are! What happens to you when you feel scared? Your heart starts to race; your palms become sweaty. There you go, a physical reaction to feeling scared! What about when you feel embarrassed? Your cheeks go red. A physical – instant – reaction. What happens when you feel nervous? Your stomach is in knots. Again, a physical symptom. Have you ever heard about people hearing shocking tragic news and throwing up straight away? That's quite a strong, immediate physical reaction.

So, it is clear that your feelings are *absolutely* connected to the physical aspects of your body. Where do your feelings come from? Your thoughts, of course! But, yet, a lot of people will still treat the mind as being completely separate from the body.

Many people say, "It's the hormones in your body" that affect the physical symptoms. Or, "It's a chemical imbalance" in the body. Now, I'm not disputing that or saying that it's *not* the hormones or the chemical imbalances that cause the physical symptoms. However, I believe that the hormones and the chemical imbalances are being produced *because* of your thoughts and feelings. Many people say a chemical imbalance in the brain causes depression. In other words, the imbalance in the brain causes you to feel sad or think depressing thoughts, and so on. But, how do you know? Which comes first, the chicken or the egg? Is it the chemical imbalance that causes the depressing thoughts or do the thoughts cause the chemical imbalance?

Let's think of a different case to help us understand this. Chemicals and hormones are one and the same in the body. So, here's an easier example. I'm borrowing this one from Deepak Chopra!

Take fear. When you are scared or afraid, your heart starts racing and you probably sweat a bit. The hormone that is produced in the body is adrenaline. Which comes first, the adrenaline - which causes the physical symptoms - or the fear? It's the fear, isn't it! You are not going to produce the adrenaline in your body unless you are in a fearful situation. The fear causes the body to produce adrenaline and the adrenaline causes the physical symptoms in the body. So, wouldn't the same be true then for *all* feelings?

If that's true, wouldn't we have to accept that loneliness and sadness might also produce physical symptoms in the body?

> *"Without the hormone, there is no feeling; without the feeling, there is no hormone. The revolution we call mind-body medicine was based on one simple fact - wherever thought goes, a chemical goes with it"*
>
> *Deepak Chopra, philosopher, endocrinologist, author*

Renowned author Louise Hay, in her book, Heal Your Body[12], links diseases with the negative mental patterns that possibly create them. It's like a dictionary for illnesses explaining for you the precise mental "stress" that you are putting your body under, which is preventing the body from doing its job and healing itself.

Surely, there are not "mental patterns" for all diseases, you're probably thinking? There are so many illnesses that are hereditary, aren't there? Interestingly, only 5% of cancer and cardiovascular disease patients can attribute their disease to heredity[13]. That means 95% of cancer patients have no "cancer gene", so where is the cancer coming from? Why is the body now no longer healing itself, as it is designed to do?

The study of a new biology called epigenetics, which literally means "control above genetics", is giving us profound insight into how the cells in our body are influenced by outside factors and are not controlled completely by DNA blueprints. Bruce H. Lipton Ph.D., in The Biology of Belief[14], tells us that, in the chromosome, the DNA forms the core, and the proteins cover the DNA like a sleeve. He says that when the genes are covered, their information cannot be "read". What is happening with the proteins in our cells is of much more importance when it comes to understanding what affects our cells.

---

12   Hay, Louise (2004), <u>Heal Your Body</u>, 4th Ed., Expanded, Rev edition, Hay House UK Ltd. (London)
13   Willett, W.C. (2002), "Balancing Life-Style and Genomics Research for Disease Prevention", 2002, <u>Science</u> 296:695-698
14   Lipton, Bruce (2008), <u>The Biology of Belief</u>, Hay House Inc. (Carlsbad)

Every cell in the body is covered with thousands of receptor proteins which respond to physical signals. According to Bruce Lipton, receptor proteins can also read vibrational energy fields such as light, sound and radio frequencies. He says that if an energy vibration in the environment resonates with a receptor's "antenna", it will alter the protein's charge, causing the receptor to change shape. Why is this important? Well, if the receptors can read energy fields, then biological behaviour can be controlled by thought as well as being controlled by physical molecules like penicillin. If a cell is bombarded with a certain energy field at a high concentration, when this particular cell decides to divide, the next cell will also have these changed receptor proteins. Think about it, this means that your regular thoughts and emotions will have a direct effect on the cells that you produce in your body which, in turn, will affect the expression of DNA in your body and can explain hereditary diseases that are linked to emotional issues passed on from mother to son/daughter, as author Louise Hay suggests.

Dr. Joe Dispenza, who studied biochemistry and whose postgraduate training is in neuroscience, brain functioning, cellular biology and aging, discusses a really fascinating point in the film, 'What the Bleep Do We Know?'. He supports the advances in epigenetics which show that it is our *reaction* to the environment that stimulates the effects of genetics that causes disease in the human body. He says that if we change our *attitude,* we're going to change the effects neurochemically, and we're going to change the effects biologically. Put simply, this changes the effects of the receptor sites and the expression of the protein and, hence, the expression of DNA in our bodies. Our attitude, he says, literally has an effect on a cellular level.

Joe says that a major factor in the aging process is poor protein production. When we age, our skin loses elasticity. Elastin is a protein. We don't digest as well. Enzymes, which aid digestion, are proteins. Our bodies and joints get stiff. Synovial fluid, the lubricant needed to reduce friction, is made up of proteins. Joe poses the question, "What happens if the muscle cell is making healthy muscle protein but, over a certain period of time, the amino acid produced from the feeling of sadness is introduced in this protein production sequence?" Well, he says, with the amino acid sequence changed, the protein is altered and this signal of the attitude is producing a cheaper grade of protein. In conclusion, he points out, because of this, the proteins that we produce when we are 16 or 17 years old are far better quality than the proteins produced when we are 50 or 60.

We all know that people look very different at different ages. We know that people often look much older than the age we know them to be. If we are bombarding our cells with certain "emotional" signals, the new cells produced from these cells will have more receptors for *these signals* and *less* for nutrients. Then, if you're eating a really great diet, but you no longer have the receptor sites after 30 years of emotional abuse to even *receive* those nutrients, does it matter what you eat? It is true that many people eat much better and healthier in their later years but, yet, their body doesn't always show these results. Did you ever think about the reasons why this might be the case?

The fantastic thing about all of this is: Since our mental attitude can cause these physical defects in our cells, it is also our mental attitude that has the power to restore them! There was a really interesting experiment carried out in Stanford University[15], where people were asked to eat something self-indulgent like a piece of chocolate cake. The people who did it with a sense of guilt and shame actually experienced a decrease in immune functioning, whereas those who were able to just enjoy the cake and the experience actually had a surge in immune status.

So, your thoughts and belief systems play a huge role in your health. Your body, if in dis-ease, manifests in physical form any emotions which are not resolved. If negative feelings are being felt continuously over a period of time or are being harboured instead of expressed, your body will try to tell you! These are feelings such as anger, resentment, bitterness, shame or the good old Irish favourite – guilt!

There is so much energy connected to feelings, after all, feelings can make you jump up and down, so if that energy isn't expressed, or released if you like, then it won't just disappear. People who never let their true feelings be expressed end up internalising them and, ultimately, those harboured feelings will make them

15   http://ezinearticles.com/?How-to-Identify-Self-Sabotaging-Patterns-and-Destroy-Them-For-Good&id=1617121

ill. Interestingly, there is a huge amount of research that connects cancer with Type C personalities. Type C personalities tend to be people pleasers, get along with everybody and never rock the boat. People who probably never say what they really feel in order to keep the peace and they can have a tendency to respond to stressful situations with a sense of hopelessness.

Think about how you feel when you have a good old cry! Isn't it true that you feel like a load has been taken off? And released? Emotional tears connected with sadness/hurt etc. contain more proteins than tears of joy or tears produced to lubricate the eyes. "Sad tears" have been found to contain the very same chemicals and enzymes that can be found in tumours and ulcers. Emotional tears contain 30 times more manganese than is found in blood, suggesting that human tear glands can concentrate and remove substances from the body. The main chemicals found in tears are: Leucine–enkephalin (a mood elevating and pain reducing endorphin), ACTH (a hormone considered to be the most reliable indicator of stress) and Prolactin (the hormone that regulates milk production in mammals). These chemicals, found in emotional tears, are hormones that build up to very high levels when the body withstands emotional stress. So, you are physically releasing toxins from your body when you let yourself express your emotions.

When you are ill, you tend to focus on every symptom and pain. Many people can get completely obsessed with their pain and illness. For some, their illness can become an integral part of their identity. People who try to be really positive and focussed on fighting their disease can get very frustrated when they do not see the physical results of this mental attitude. Often, this is because their focus is on *fighting the disease*. However, remember how our reality works: we draw to us the very thing we think about most. You get in life what you focus on. So, when you are unwell, you need to be focusing all your thoughts and energies on *health!* If your focus is on *fighting the disease*, it is still on the disease and not on health!

Has it happened to you before that you were really tired or not feeling great and your friends made plans to go out? Suddenly, you felt much better and were really up for the night out! It's amazing how we can heal ourselves if the motivation is there or the distraction is strong enough.

Also, you've got to watch out for those beliefs connected to our health that we have chosen for ourselves and constantly affirm:

"I always get the flu in winter."

Or

"I get three colds a year."

"I always get sick on holiday."

"I'll always suffer from a bad back!"

> *"In order to permanently eliminate a condition, we must first work to dissolve*

the mental cause. The symptom is only an outer effect. When the need is gone, the outer effect must die. Our consistent thinking patterns create our experiences. Therefore, by changing our thinking patterns, we can change our experiences"

Louise Hay, author

Part 2

Techniques & Practical Strategies

Chapter 11

AWARENESS IS KEY

We have looked at attitudes, outlooks and mindsets that produce success *in life.* We've looked at how the mind works and how it can impact your behaviour, your reality, the things you attract into your life and your body. Learning about how the mind works gives us a better understanding of how to look after it.

In this section, I want to share with you some helpful techniques and strategies that will help you *apply* the information you've read in Part 1 so that you can understand how to start to put it into practice. I've used this quote before but I want to put it in here again because understanding it is very important.

> **"What you are aware of, you are in control of. What you are unaware of, is in control of you."**
>
> *Anthony de Mello, Jesuit priest and psychotherapist*

First technique: Watch your thoughts

> *"People become really quite remarkable when they start thinking that they can do things. When they believe in themselves, they have the first secret of success"*
>
> *Dr. Norman Vincent Peale, minister and author*

Awareness is the first step. Becoming aware of the things that you do that *hinder* your progress is the first step to changing the way you think. At first, just become conscious of *how* you speak to yourself. Step outside of yourself and listen to your mental chatter. How often is your mental chatter positive and how often is it negative? Do you give yourself mixed messages?

Listen out for those statements that are damaging. Always ask yourself, "Would I say something like that to a friend whom I'm helping become a better happier person?" We've learnt, from Part 1, how much negative comments can affect behaviour, and we have to then realise that when we do it to ourselves, it's not going to be any different, we will negatively affect our *own* behaviour.

The problem is, we don't think! We don't think about what we say to ourselves at all. We let it run on like background noise and, it's only when we stop to take notice of it, we realise how constantly negative it can be.

How can you expect to become the best possible version of you if you continue to speak to yourself in that way? We often think that we cannot control the thoughts that come into our head, but that's untrue! We have a choice. You may feel that the thought jumps into your head out of your control but, at that point, you make a decision. You can *choose* to continue thinking that thought or you can *choose* to think something different. We often think, "Oh, everyone speaks negatively to themselves". It's not true, successful happy people do not talk down to themselves. In fact, they do the opposite; they constantly use their mental chatter to pump themselves up!

Do you *want* to do something but, in your head, there's a running commentary, "I can't do it, I can't do it, I can't do it"? It's like buying a ticket to go to a concert and then getting in the taxi and telling the driver to drive to the cinema! When you become aware of this, you realise how silly it is to continue doing the very thing you *know* is going to hold you back. Be your own best friend and speak to yourself in a way that will help you achieve your ultimate goal in life, your happiness.

> *"If you put a small value upon yourself, rest assured that the world will not raise your price"*
>
> *Anon*

Second Technique: Write down the thoughts you *want* to be thinking

> *"If you want to reach a state of bliss, then go beyond your ego and the internal dialogue. Make a decision to relinquish the need to control, the need to be approved, and the need to judge. Those are the three things the ego is doing all the time. It's very important to be aware of them every time they come up"*
>
> Deepak Chopra, philosopher, endocrinologist, author

What way would you like to speak to yourself on a regular basis? What are the thoughts that you would like to think automatically? You need to start to re-train your thinking! And it's got to start off consciously. You may be re-training 15 or 20 years' of speaking to yourself in a certain way so it mightn't happen overnight - but it *will* happen.

Think about anything you have ever learned to do. First of all, every little step is conscious. Think about what it's like when you learn how to drive. You have to learn to check mirrors, use the clutch and the gearstick, and watch everything on the road. With practice, all the techniques you learn start to become really natural to you. This is how we learn any new skill. First, we are consciously incompetent (we're aware we cannot do it). Then, we become consciously competent (we're aware of all the skills to do it). And, soon, we are unconsciously competent (we do the skills so naturally and automatically often without even thinking about it).

So, start writing down the things that you would like to think. How would you like to react to situations? What would you like your mental chatter to sound like? Become aware of the changes you want to make.

> *"You, yourself, as much as anybody in the entire universe, deserve your love and affection"*
>
> *Buddha*

Third Technique: Watch out for your limiting beliefs!

"To know the true reality of yourself, you must be aware not only of your conscious thoughts, but also of your unconscious beliefs, prejudices, bias and habits"

Anon

The more aware you become of your mental chatter and your thoughts, the more you will start to catch yourself saying things that you suddenly realise are attitudes or beliefs that are really not good ones to have. These could be old sayings that your mum or granddad used to say that you took on board and you probably never really questioned how thinking them may be holding you back.

Remember, your beliefs create your life. They will affect what circumstances you draw into your world and how you perceive the situations around you. I'm not talking about religious beliefs here but the beliefs that are created from a repeated thought pattern. That's all a belief is, a repeated thought.

Here are a few examples of some limiting beliefs you may have:

"Nothing in life comes easy."

"People are out to get me."

"Life is dangerous."

"You can't trust anyone."

"I'm not good enough."

"Money is the root of all evil."

"Don't expect too much and you'll never be disappointed."

"If I get angry, I'm a bad person."

"Illness runs in our family."

"Money always goes out faster than it comes in."

When a limiting belief pops into your head - stop it! Immediately choose a positive thought to replace it. In time, your new thought will replace that automatic old limiting belief.

> *"The only limits we have in life are those that we place on ourselves!"*
>
> *Anon*

Fourth Technique: *Intend* the day to go as you wish

> *"On waking in the morning, confirm your intention that your day will be magnificent! As you are creating every one of your days, if you don't intend your day in advance, then you're handing it over to the whims and energies of mass consciousness. Don't put your day in the hands of others- create your own magnificent day!"*

> *Rhonda Byrne, author of The Secret*

We have seen in Part 1 that research now shows that not only do your thoughts affect your own behaviour and the way you see things, but they also impact your reality. Happy, successful people always focus on what it is they *want* to happen.

In the mornings, take a couple of minutes to *intend* your day to go well. Visualise the day as you wish it to go. It is amazing how much this has an effect on your day. Just start off with the intention. *Intend* to have a great day. *Intend* everything to go smoothly. *Intend* to feel good. Focus on what it is you want and imagine it to be that way.

This is a really powerful technique but, if you don't buy it, then do the following.

One morning before you get out of bed, spend about five to ten minutes affirming that the day will be a really good day, that you are in great form, that the day is running really smoothly and everything falls into place. Really put the effort into this. Run through a movie in your mind of everything going smoothly for you during the day, of you laughing and having a joke with your friends and of you feeling really good. The next morning, do nothing, just get up and go about your day as normal. On the third day, reflect on how different the two days were for you - I guarantee you'll have found a difference!

> *"Never mind what is. Imagine it the way you want it to be so that your vibration is a match to your desire. When your vibration is a match to your desire, all things in your experience will gravitate to meet that every match every time"*
>
> *Esther Hicks, inspirational speaker and author*

Fifth Technique: List the things you are grateful for!

***"When you are grateful, fear disappears
and abundance appears"***

Anthony Robbins, life coach and author

Being grateful is a very important trait. You should always be working on it. The reason? Well, you will never meet a happy person who isn't grateful! Think about it. Think about any happy people you know. These two traits go hand-in-hand and are pretty inseparable. You will not find a happy person who is not grateful and you will not find a truly grateful person who is not happy!

Listing, in detail (the more detail, the better the feeling), the things that you are grateful for automatically puts you in a better mood. It's interesting to see how long it takes you the first time you do this as you might initially find it quite difficult. It'll be a good indication of how grateful a person you are starting off.

Begin by listing 25 things for which you are grateful. The more you do this, the easier it becomes because it opens the doors of appreciation. The more you think about the things for which you are grateful, the more appreciative you become. And the more appreciative you become, the more you see things differently around you. I do this technique every single day. And I know that because I focus on the things for which I'm grateful, the more I draw similar things into my life. I have trained myself to become so much more grateful and appreciative that now it's my automatic reaction to things.

We often forget to be grateful about things. We regularly worry and worry about certain things/events and when it turns out that they don't happen, we don't even bother to appreciate that what we were worrying about *hasn't* happened. We don't even say, "Oh, thank goodness". We just go straight onto the next thing that might happen and start worrying about that!

A happy person is a grateful person and, when you start to see the world with appreciative eyes, wonderful things can happen.

> *"Whatever we think about and thank about, we bring about"*
>
> *Dr. John F. Demartini, human behavioural specialist and author*

Sixth Technique: Collate a tool box of mood changers

> *"There is only one person who could ever make you happy, and that person is you"*
>
> *Dr. David Burns, psychiatry professor*

Happy, successful people understand that it is YOU and only YOU who can control your own happiness and mood. Sometimes, we can be in a bad mood because we're angry at someone. If you are experiencing a feeling, it's very important that you express it (just don't forget to let it go once it's expressed!). However, how many times have you been in a bad mood for no reason? Have you ever been in an 'off' mood and not known why?

When you can't think of any reason for your mood, then perhaps it wasn't your mood! Perhaps it's just a way you've learned to "be" or, perhaps, you're picking up the frequencies from the environment you are in. Remember, if we are not in control of it, then it has control over us. Is your state just a reaction to the whims of others or the energies of mass consciousness?

Have you ever thought about what things put you in a good mood? Being in a good mood automatically means you are vibrating on a higher frequency and so having a "bank" of mood changers can completely turn your day around. Keeping yourself on a higher frequency means you are always drawing things of a similar frequency into your life.

I'm going to share with you three of mine.

o   I watch my favourite programme ever, 'Friends'! This never fails to put a smile on my face. In fact, I *always* put it on when I have to tackle a very untidy house! Whenever the house is a mess where I have loads to do and the thought of it is putting me in a bad mood, I stick on 'Friends' in the background (I only need to hear the dialogue since I know all the episodes so well) and it's the perfect distraction while I'm doing chores. Before I know it, I have all my work done and I'm in a good mood! First thing in the morning, I am also very aware that I don't want to be influenced unconsciously in a negative way, so I always put on light-hearted fun TV and never the news. That way, I always start my day off smiling! I wait and listen to the news later in the morning when I am in control of my state and so will not let myself be influenced by negative media coverage.

o   The second one I stole from the US TV show, 'Ally McBeal'. In one episode, her therapist (I think) advised her to find a really powerful song that made her feel really good. She told her to play it in her head every time she felt she needed a boost. This one really works! We all know what a fantastic mood enhancer music is. I have a CD mix full of songs that are really strong 'feel good' songs. I play it most mornings in the car on the way to work and it really sets me up for a great day. A song that you love will always act as a trigger for your unconscious mind and will automatically transport you back to the emotional state you have associated with that song.

o   Be around people who make you feel good. Even if you are tired and in an "odd" mood, accept that invitation from friends to go out for a walk. You know your mood will change after about five minutes in their company. Surrounding yourself with people who always boost your energy and frequency is very important. There are plenty of people who "drain" you and you must be careful not to let *their* habitual state affect yours. Just being aware of this can often be enough for you to be able to control how much of *their* state affects you. However, these people often need a time limit and don't be afraid to enforce one! Some of my "energy" boosters are: my little goddaughter, who just has to mutter the words, "Auntie Clair"; my husband, who always knows what to say to make me laugh; and my little doggie, a head tilt with those brown eyes and I melt!

"It's really important that you feel good.
Because this feeling good is what goes
out as a signal into the universe and
starts to attract more of itself to you.
So, the more you can feel good, the more
you will attract the things that help you
feel good and that will keep bringing
you up higher and higher"

Dr. Joe Vitale, metaphysician

Chapter 12

FOCUS ON WHAT YOU WANT

"You give birth to that on which you fix your mind"

Antoine de Saint Exupery, writer

We know from Part 1 that you get in life what you focus on. So, it's really important that you **know** what you want to focus on. Have you ever really sat down and given yourself some time to think about what it is that you really want? Have you ever given yourself time to really focus on how you want your life to be? Have you ever really thought about what it is that you actually want in life? What are the things that will make you happy? Very few people do this. And, yet, when you think about it, if we really want to be happy in life, how can we *not* do it?

Many young people find it really hard to know what they want to do with their lives and they often get seduced by the idea of being famous. And the reason for the fame doesn't seem to matter at all. Be careful, fame doesn't mean happiness, as we discussed at the very beginning of the book. So, how do you know what you want?

A really good technique is to consider the same type of question as asked in Chapter 1. If you feel that fame and money are important to you, ask yourself: If you had plenty of money and everyone recognised and loved you, what would you still want to *do* in your life? The answer might take a little while to come to you, but just keep focussing your mind back to the question and take the *time* to think about the things that will make you happy.

> *"Learn to become still. And take your attention away from what you don't want, and all the emotional charge around it, and place your attention on what you wish to experience"*
>
> *Rev. Dr. Michael Beckwith, visionary*

Seventh Technique: Set your goals on what you want

"What you get by achieving your goals
is not as important as what you become
by achieving your goals"

Goethe, writer

Sit down and allocate at least 20 minutes to think about your life and what it is that you really want. Picture it, imagine what it would look like, sound like, and feel like! Have you ever thought about *why* it is that people set goals? What is the purpose of setting targets or goals for ourselves? It is, of course, to *motivate* us. In order to do this well, I want to share with you some strategies you should know about effective goal-setting. In order for your conscious and unconscious mind to really take on board the goals that you want for yourself, you should make sure they are written in such a way that they are SMART.

S Short and Specific. If your goals are really long-winded and vague, it is going to be much less likely for you to be able to achieve them. Your unconscious mind appreciates clear instructions, so your goals must be really clear and very specific about what you want.

M Meaningful and Measurable. It's no surprise that you will be less likely to achieve your goals if they don't really mean something to you, but it is worth emphasising this. So often, we can allow ourselves to set goals that are really more for other people than for us. So, it is important to highlight that your personal goals should be all about what you want for you. The other 'M' is a very important psychological factor in goal-setting. The goal must be measurable, otherwise how will you know when you have achieved it? Take an example of, "My goal is to be happy". How can you measure that? How will you know when you're happy? That goal is neither clear nor specific and really cannot be measured, so your mind will have trouble digesting this one!

A Achievable and "As If Now". It is important that your goal is achievable because, if not, you will not be able to truly believe that it is possible for you. We know that if your thoughts and beliefs are not coherent, there is no way that your goals will manifest. This is not saying that you cannot dream big. Not at all! It just means that you need to *believe* it's achievable. Some people have a great innate skill of having the belief for really big and wonderful things. As long as you are really open to the fact that this is possible for you then the goal is achievable for you. "As If Now" is another great little trick for your unconscious mind. When you are writing down your goals, write them as if they are happening now. That means, write them in the present tense. You're probably wondering why this may be necessary. But try it ... take one of your goals, make sure it is specific, meaningful, measurable, achievable, then put it in the present tense. I'll show you an example:

"I hope to get an A in Maths."

Now change it to:

"I am getting an A in Maths."

Say it out loud! Which one makes it *feel* more possible?

John Assaraf explains that when you say your goals with, "I hope" or "I wish", the rest of the unfinished thought, whether conscious or unconscious, is "I bet I won't" or "I bet I can't". He says, if you don't believe it will happen, it is almost guaranteed that it won't!

R Realistic and Responsible. Your goals must be realistic and real for you. They must also be responsible. For example, say you want a brilliant social life and your focus is then on socialising and being out with friends. You have to think about your goals carefully. Do you want a brilliant social life? If you have one, what might suffer? And will you be truly happy if other things suffer just for your fantastic social life? Wouldn't a more responsible goal be to have more of a balanced social life? Always question whether achieving the goal you set for yourself will truly be the best thing for you.

T Timed and Toward. A bit like "Measurable", time is an important one for your unconscious mind to really have the clear instruction on how and when to achieve your goal. I'll use the example from earlier: *It is August 20??* (put in the year) *and my results show I am getting an A in Maths.* This is really making the goal clear and precise for you.

Your goal should also be a *toward* goal.

Toward & Away Goals!

How are you motivated? Towards something or away from something? Let me use the good old example of tidying your room! Do you tidy because you like your room tidy? And knowing that it is going to look tidy motivates you to tidy? Or do you tidy just to avoid it being in a complete mess? Does it have to get in a real state before you get motivated to tidy? Which one are you? The first one is a Toward goal, the second an Away goal. So, what's the big deal, you're probably thinking. Both get the job done. The key thing here is all about (i) your focus (ii) your motivation.

How many people make a New Year's Resolution to get fit and healthy? Let's try and understand these in terms of Toward and Away goals. The Toward goal is, "I am fit and healthy". The Away goal is, "I don't want to be bloated and lethargic!" If your motivation is to *not* feel bloated and lethargic then, yes, that'll get you started. You will move away from being bloated and lethargic and probably get a start on a half-decent exercise regime. However, the more you move away from being bloated and lethargic, the more you are going to lose your motivation, since your motivation is, after all, from feeing bloated and lethargic! You're not quite where you really want to be, but you are moving further and further away from your motivation. Your unconscious mind is programmed to always seek more and more, so your mind is going to *need* and be *drawn back* to your motivation. So, after you make some moves in the right direction, soon, you're going to find yourself right back to being bloated and lethargic! And then, HEY HO, you'll get all motivated again!

If your goal and full focus was on what you really wanted, that is, to be fit and healthy, then your motivation would last until you achieved it. You wouldn't be drawn back to something else for motivation because, if your motivation is being fit and healthy, then you're going to stay on track until you're fit and healthy!

So, this is the psychology behind goal-setting. Your mind needs a Toward focus. This comes from the fact that your mind cannot process negatives directly. Did you know that? Your mind is like a computer, there are no opposites, just a number of alternatives. Have you ever been somewhere with a friend and they say to you, "Don't look now but ..." And what do you do? You look, before you've really processed what's she's said, like some instinctive reaction, you've looked before she's even finished the sentence. This is because your mind cannot process the, "Don't Look" directly. In other words it, first of all, has to understand what it means *to look* before it can process what it means *not to look.*

So, set your goals, think about exactly what you want. You have probably never sat down and done that before. Successful people always do this. They know exactly what they want and have given a lot of focus and energy on that end product. So much so, they know exactly what they're doing at every point because it is always working towards their ultimate goal. For them, everything they do has a powerful purpose.

"The reason most people never reach their goals is that they don't define them, or even seriously consider them as believable or achievable. Winners can tell you where they are going, what they plan to do along the way, and who will be sharing the adventure with them"

Dr Denis Waitley, motivational speaker and author

Eighth Technique: Stretch your mind

"Man's mind, once stretched by a new idea, never regains its original dimensions"

Oliver Wendell Holmes, writer

When you think a thought, it creates a neural pathway in your brain. Repeatedly thinking that thought will strengthen that neural pathway. When you think a thought that is different to your usual way of thinking, then you create a new neural pathway in the brain. The same happens with a new experience. Years ago, psychologists and scientists believed that by the time you're a teenager, you will have created *all* your neural pathways associated with *your* thinking. They believed that they are then "hardwired" and set in place for how you will deal with everything that comes your way in the future. However, neuroscientists have now discovered that the number of potential connections your brain can make over your lifetime is about one followed by six million zeros. However, if after a certain age, we refuse to look at things in different ways or we are stubborn in our mind-sets, then we will never create new neural pathways in our brains and this ultimately limits us greatly.

Our body doesn't always react well to these new neural pathways. Sometimes when we move outside our comfort zone, our body sees this as a threat. Whether the move be a good thing for us or a bad thing for us, our survival instincts say, "Hey this is different, you need to be careful". This is why repetition is very important when creating a new thought pattern or habit. Just like any new habit, it takes about 26 to 30 days of conscious effort before something feels like it is natural to us. The same goes for making new neural pathways. This eighth technique will help you accept new neural pathways easier.

Paul McKenna describes this really well in his book, "I can make you rich".[16] He explains this particular technique when helping this guy change the way he thought about money. This particular guy was complaining that, in order to make as much money as he wanted, he would need to work 350 days a year. He currently charged £120 a day for his training services. Paul suggested that he charge £1,200 for the day on the next proposal he sent out. The man looked at him, astonished! He could not comprehend sending out a proposal for £1,200 for one day's work. After watching him struggle with this for a few moments, Paul said, "OK, why don't you just charge double what you used to. Worst case, they'll just negotiate you back down to your normal rate." The guy smiled and thought, "Yeah, I could do that."

But here's the thing. If Paul had suggested to him at the beginning to double his rate, he would've found *that* difficult. But once his mind had been sufficiently stretched, it would never return to its original limitations. What is the difference between you and a financially successful person? You think about your worth in much lower denominations. And the key difference is that all

---

16   McKenna, Paul, (2007), I Can Make You Rich, Bantam Press (London)

wealthy people *think* about money in very different ways.

So, when thinking about your goals and what it is you want - stretch your thinking! Initially, think about something you'd consider impossible. Stretch your mind really far and then gradually bring it back closer (but still beyond) your own reality. The more you do this, the less you'll feel the impossible is impossible!

> *"Nimble thought can jump both sea and land"*
>
> *Shakespeare*

Ninth Technique: Make a Vision Board

> *"Ordinary people believe only in the possible. Extraordinary people visualise not what is possible or probable but rather what is impossible. And by visualising the impossible, they begin to see it as possible"*
>
> *Dr. Cherie Carter Scott, motivational speaker and author*

Visualisation is a technique that is used by people all over the world. Many athletes use it as a part of their preparation and it is a key component of NASA training. Why?

It works!

Your unconscious brain responds best to symbols (after all, it's how your unconscious communicates with you through dreams). So, by using mental pictures and movies, your unconscious mind understands much clearer what you are looking to draw into your life. So, how does that work? Well, did you know that the brain cannot differentiate between something that is "run through" in your mind and something that you actually physically do? The same neural pathways are sparked whether you are just visualising it happening or whether you are actually are doing it.

John Assaraf, in his quest for the science behind why all these strategies and techniques work, provides us with more insight. He explains that our brains work like Google. When we have a set of neural pathways and patterns of thinking hardwired into our brains, as explained in the previous section, our brains will edit out all the billions of bits of information that's irrelevant to our needs/values. Remember in the chapter, 'What way are we seeing things today?', we discussed how we see the world based on our beliefs and thinking. This is why! Our brains will filter out the data that is not coherent with how our pathways are wired up.

John explains this really well with the example of a mother and her child. A mother waiting outside school gates will hear all the cries from all the children running out the school doors but, when her own child cries, she will hear that cry out of all the other sounds and will only focus on her own child's cries. Why? Because she recognises that sound pattern and she has programmed herself to filter out all the rest. Have you ever really wanted to buy a pair of shoes but say, you couldn't afford them, but then everywhere you go you see people wearing those shoes! It's because it was put into your very own Google search engine, so your brain filters out all other information and hones in on that very bit on which you had been focussing. Neuroscientists call this search engine your Reticular Activation System. They say that your reticular formation picks up all the sensory input from your environment and, if it's important to you, it sends a signal to your conscious brain to alert you that something of interest to you is going on. It does this at a speed 800 times faster than your conscious brain cells operate. Amazing, right? Well, as John explains, this can be a blessing or a curse. If you are focussing on what you don't want, then your very own Google search engine will filter out all other information and give you exactly that – what you don't want.

Have you ever been worried about missing a bus? What goes through your mind? No doubt your mental chatter is going something like, "Oh no, I'm going to miss the bus; I'm running late, I'm not going to make it..." But what about the pictures in your mind? I bet in your mind you're actually picturing a movie of you missing the bus. You are actually visualising yourself missing the bus!

You need to "wire" your brain so that what you are inputting is exactly what you want. This is where visualisation comes in. By putting the information very clearly into your "search engine", using the very form your unconscious mind recognises best - images and movies - then you are giving your brain the clear signal of what it needs to search for.

A vision board is a really great activity that will keep you visualising your life as you want it. Take a large corkboard and on it, put images related to your goals. You'll find plenty of examples of vision boards on the internet. This activity is so much fun because it gets you excited about the future. Put this board up in your room or somewhere you are going to see it every day. Take time everyday to look at and imagine what it would be like having all of those things *now.*

Visualise what it is like achieving your goals. The more effort you put into the visualisation, the better and the quicker it will work for you. The feelings you have when you look at that board are extremely important. If you have an underlying feeling (belief) that this won't work, then you're giving yourself mixed messages. Your brain cannot work for you if you are giving it mixed signals about what you want or do not believe is possible.

"When you visualise, then you materialise. If you've been there in the mind, you'll go there in the body"

Dr Denis Waitley, motivational speaker and author

Tenth Technique: Accept responsibility

> **"We are each responsible for all our experiences"**
>
> *Louise Hay, author*

This tenth technique is the ability to *really* accept responsibility for everything that goes on in our lives. As a human race, we love to blame but, as explained in Chapter 3, you cannot make positive changes if you are on the 'Effect' side. This means truly understanding that your life is a reflection of you. Everything in your life is giving you feedback about you.

This technique isn't the easiest but will be one of the most powerful. When you are constantly on the 'Cause' side, you are always open to new learning and opportunities. When you are not open to these and you are on the 'Effect' side, your life will start to repeat itself until the learning occurs. You see, as psychologists tell us, your life is full of patterns and cycles. You will repeat a pattern until a change inside you occurs. A change on the inside will produce a change on the outside. This is why the woman who was abused by her first husband often finds herself attracted to another man who also ends up abusing her. Or why couples will often have the same argument over and over.

Reflect on your life. Have you ever asked yourself, "Why does this always happen to me?" Then, do you have a repeating pattern? You have to ask yourself, when the situation is presenting itself again and again but perhaps in different contexts and with different people, what is the common denominator? If *you* are the cause, then *you* are the one with all the power to change your life!

And so, if our thoughts affect how we see the world and what we draw into our lives, is there such a thing as a coincidence? Everything happens for a reason- and the reason is YOU! Events or people are either a lesson or a blessing, and so the reason is always for YOU!

YOU are in charge; YOU are the director of your life! We go through life often not understanding how much we stand in the way of our own success and happiness. We focus on what we don't want instead of what we want. We think about things that make us feel bad. We think that we have no control over our own thoughts. We talk down to ourselves on a regular basis. We give ourselves mixed messages. We don't understand that it all boils down to what we *choose* to believe. And what we *choose* to think. That key fundamental process can make or break you. And it all really comes down to this one question:

So what do you think?

Printed in the United States
By Bookmasters